The story of the 6

the Durham Light Infantry

$b France, April 1915-November 1918

Sir Ralph Bignell Ainsworth

Alpha Editions

This edition published in 2024

ISBN : 9789362993564

Design and Setting By
Alpha Editions
www.alphaedis.com
Email - info@alphaedis.com

Contents

FOREWORD.

During one of the short periods of training in 1917, it was suggested that lectures should be delivered to the troops on the history of their battalions in France. Accordingly Capt. G. Kirkhouse, then Assistant Adjutant, set to work to collect material for this purpose. Owing to there being no officers, and very few men, who had served continuously with the Battalion since April, 1915, the task was not easy, and it was found impossible to complete the information in time for a lecture before the Battalion returned to the line. The material was carefully preserved, however, and was the only portion of the records which survived the disaster of the 27th May, 1918. As soon as time permitted, the task was continued, but owing to there being very few survivors of earlier days, many details have probably escaped notice. Imperfect and incomplete as the story is, however, it is hoped that the details related will serve to recall other incidents, both pleasant and unpleasant, to those members of the Battalion who have been fortunate enough to survive.

It is regretted that it has not been found practicable to include a chapter on the inner life of the Battalion which centred round the characters of some of its members. So many names occur to one's mind that a chapter would be inadequate to mention all, and the exclusion of any would have involved an invidious and unjustifiable selection.

R.B.A.

July, 1919.

CHAPTER I.
THE "SALIENT."

First Phase.

The end of March, 1915, found the 50th (Northumbrian) Division of the Territorial Force awaiting orders to proceed overseas. The infantry of the Division consisted of the 149th Infantry Brigade (4th, 5th, 6th and 7th Battalions Northumberland Fusiliers), the 150th Infantry Brigade (4th Battalion East Yorkshire Regiment, 4th and 5th Battalions Yorkshire Regiment, and 5th Battalion The Durham Light Infantry), and the 151st Infantry Brigade (6th, 7th, 8th and 9th Battalions The Durham Light Infantry). Early in April, when the 6th Battalion The Durham Light Infantry were in billets at Gateshead, the orders arrived and on the 10th April Capt. F. Walton proceeded to Havre to make arrangements for the arrival of the transport section. The first detachment of men to leave Gateshead consisted of the transport and machine-gun sections which, under Major J.E. Hawdon, Second in Command, and Lieut. H.T. Bircham, Transport Officer, entrained at the Cattle Market, Newcastle, on the 17th April for Southampton, en route for Havre.

Two days later the remainder of the Battalion entrained at the Central Station, Newcastle, with the following officers: Lieut.-Col. H.C. Watson in command, Capt. J.W. Jeffreys, Adjutant; Major W.M. Mackay, Medical Officer; Capt. A.P. Cummins, commanding A Company; Major S.E. Badcock, commanding B Company; Capt. W.H.D. Devey, commanding C Company; and Capt. J. Townend, commanding D Company. Arriving at Folkestone the same day, the Battalion embarked for Boulogne, where it arrived about midnight and marched up to Ostrohove Camp.

The following day it entrained at Pont de Briques Station, on the train which brought the transport and machine-gun sections from Havre. The complete battalion detrained at Cassel, and after marching all night arrived in billets at Hardifort at 5 a.m. on the 21st April.

On the 23rd April orders were received to march at very short notice to Steenvoorde, where the whole of the 151st Infantry Brigade, commanded at this time by Brig.-General Martin, was assembled in a field at the eastern end of the town. During the remainder of the day the men were allowed to rest. At dusk two battalions of the Brigade, the 7th and 9th Battalions, marched off in fighting order. The other two Battalions (the 6th and 8th) proceeded by 'buses through Poperinghe to Vlamertinghe, where they took over a hut camp recently vacated by the 9th Royal Scots.

It was now evident that the lessons which the Battalion had learnt during its long period of training were very soon to be put into practice. The 24th April was spent in testing rifles and making final preparations for action, and in the evening an order arrived from the Brigade to get ready to move quickly. This order was given out and within half an hour the Battalion was on the pavé road, marching towards Ypres. It entered the town as night settled on it. At this date the town was not ruined and the results of the shelling were hardly noticeable. As the Battalion was passing the Cloth Hall a shell came screaming faintly towards it, and, passing over, burst with a dull roar in the city a quarter of a mile away. There had been no talking in the ranks nor any sound except the beat of ammunition boots on the pavé, but when this shell screamed overhead and burst, ejaculation in the good old Durham tongue could be heard passing cheerily up the length of the column. Two or three more shells passed over, but none burst near the Battalion.

Reaching the top of the hill to the east of the city and leaving the white walls of Potijze Château on the left, the Battalion turned off the road and filed into the G.H.Q. line, a Battalion of the Shropshire Light Infantry climbing out to make room. This trench was of the breastwork type, and a novelty to the men whose idea of a trench was a ditch below the ground level. The dispositions of the Battalion were as follows: A Company were on the south side of the Potijze road and the remainder on the north side, with B Company on the right, D Company in the centre, and C Company on the left. The machine-gun section was with D Company. Transport lines were established just behind the Château near to a Canadian Battery. The position was unfortunate, for the section came under heavy shell fire and had several men and horses hit.

Sunday, the 25th April, was the first day spent by the Battalion in the trenches. There was a considerable amount of shelling, but fortunately the Battalion in the trenches did not suffer. In the evening, as it got dark, the Battalion moved out of the trench and, forming up on the road which it had left the previous night, marched in fours for about a mile to Velorenhoek village, which was then almost intact. There the Battalion came under the orders of the 85th Infantry Brigade, and halted. All ranks slept for some hours on the roadside, or in the fields, gardens or cottages close to the road. Before dawn the Brigadier ordered the Battalion to vacate the village, and the column moved a few hundred yards up the road to the east. Here the Companies left the road and the men improved with their entrenching tools the little cover in the form of ditches and trenches which was to be found, and then lay down. Throughout this and the succeeding days the men were in marching order with full packs. The transport moved back to Potijze Wood, except the ration limbers, which went back to Poperinghe.

About 10 a.m. on the 26th word was passed for the Commanding Officer and Adjutant, who accordingly reported to the Brigadier of the 85th Brigade. He was standing on the north side of the road on a little rising ground from which there was a view for a mile or two to the eastward. He gave the following order verbally: "The Germans have broken through our line and are advancing south-west. The Durham Light Infantry (6th Battalion) will advance and take up positions between Zonnebeke level crossing and Hill 37." He described the position of the crossing, later known as Devil's Crossing, by pointing out the direction and stated that the hill with a few trees on it to the E.N.E. was Hill 37. He further stated that the Shropshire Light Infantry would be on the right and that Lieut.-Colonel Bridgford, of that Regiment, would be in command of the 6th Battalion.

Orders were accordingly issued to Company Commanders verbally by the Adjutant as follows: The Battalion is to occupy the line between Hill 37, which can be seen on the left front, and Zonnebeke crossing, which lies on the road. Captain Cummins's Company (A) will march on the crossing and Captain Townend's Company (D) on Hill 37. Major Badcock's Company (B) and Captain Devey's Company (C) will divide the space between. Advance in artillery formation, take advantage of the cover afforded by the ground, and each Company Commander should accompany one of his rear Platoons. When Companies had gained suitable positions on this line they were to deploy and attack by fire any bodies of the enemy who might attempt to cross their front. The whole operation was under direct observation by enemy balloons, and as soon as the Companies moved an intense barrage was put down. B Company, on the right, however, had a comparatively good time and suffered very few casualties, whilst No. 5 Platoon, under Lieut. A.B. Hare, had none at all, and reached Zonnebeke Crossing in safety. The remaining Companies got the full effect of the barrage, which included gas shells, and lost direction towards the left. Capt. W.H.D. Devey, commanding C Company, was wounded, Capt. J. Monkhouse killed, and 2nd Lieut. H.H. Nicholson wounded. As a result of the loss of direction a gap was formed, and A Company were pushed forward to fill it. In spite of heavy casualties the line was maintained, and continued to advance, firing all the time on the enemy, who could be seen from the new positions. It was not till they had advanced a considerable distance that the officers and men found that there was another line of British troops ahead of them, holding out in shell-holes, on hillsides, etc.

When this was discovered, Lieut. T.B. Heslop, with No. 11 Platoon and part of No. 9 Platoon, joined the London Rifle Brigade; 2nd Lieut. R.V. Hare, with No. 10 Platoon, joined a Battalion of the Shropshire Light

Infantry, and 2nd Lieut. G. Angus, with the remainder of No. 9 Platoon, took up a position in support on the hill. By this time A and D Companies were in the forward positions. As already described, A Company had moved up to fill the gap between B and C Companies, and D Company had also moved to the assistance of C Company. As a result, the men of all Companies were mixed together, and it is difficult to say how they were distributed, but A Company seem to have been in two parts, one with D Company and one next to B Company. The former passed over Hill 37 and eventually joined the London Rifle Brigade in some ditches which formed the front line. There they suffered many casualties. Amongst others, Major S.E. Badcock and 2nd Lieut. Kynoch were killed and Capt. F. Walton and 2nd Lieut. G. Kirkhouse were wounded. As soon as the advance had commenced, the Adjutant, Capt. J.W. Jeffreys, had galloped through the barrage to find Zonnebeke crossing. Having shown it to the Company on the right flank he proceeded along the line and found a Platoon of D Company under 2nd Lieut. Lyon digging themselves in. A little further along another Platoon was found, and whilst showing them the line he was heavily fired on. After returning to Brigade Headquarters for a fresh horse he went to Hill 37 and there heard of D Company from some men of the Rifle Brigade. Before dusk all formed parties had got into touch with Battalion Headquarters, which were at Zevencote barn, beside Zonnebeke level crossing.

About 4 p.m. Lt.-Col. Bridgford, who was in command of all troops in this sector, issued orders for an attack to be made to clear the enemy from the Fortuin-Passchendaele Road. The attack was to be made by two Companies of the Shropshire Light Infantry, with the 7th Durham Light Infantry in support and the 6th in reserve. The attacking troops were to pass through the front line and establish a new line on the road when captured. A conference of officers was held, and it was ascertained that the men available for the attack were as follows:—No. 3 Platoon under 2nd Lieut. Blenkinsop, Nos. 5, 7 and 8 Platoons, under Capt. T. Welch, with Lieuts. A.B. Hare and H.C.W. Haythornthwaite; No. 9 Platoon under 2nd Lieut. G. Angus, and about forty men of D Company under Capt. J. Townend and 2nd Lieut. P.H.B. Lyon.

The Battalion, which was lying in a trench near the road, began to advance about 7 or 8 p.m., moving in artillery formation and following the 7th Durham Light Infantry towards the ridge to the north of Zonnebeke.

On reaching the ridge, which was found unoccupied, the 7th Battalion moved off to Zonnebeke and the 6th Battalion was ordered to send three Companies to the support of the Hampshire Regiment on Gravenstafel Ridge further to the north.

In accordance with the orders issued by Lt.-Col. Hicks, commanding the Hampshires, B Company, who were about 90 strong, left the remainder of the Battalion, who were now at Hicks' Farm and moved to reinforce 2nd Lieut. Ball of the Royal Fusiliers (28th Div.), who, with 100 men, was holding a position on the Gravenstafel Ridge. This position consisted of a much battered breastwork, of which only isolated portions offered any cover. The remainder of the Battalion was then divided. C Company were sent to garrison a strong point near a neighbouring farm, leaving No. 9 Platoon, under 2nd Lieut. G. Angus, to form a ration party. A Company was held in reserve in isolated trenches. Battalion Headquarters and D Company moved back to Zevencote barn, where the Company occupied some trenches.

On the night of the 27th April, A Company with about twenty men of D Company were sent to fill a gap between the Hampshires and the Shropshires, where they dug themselves in. The following day Capt. A.P. Cummins and Capt. D. Park were seriously wounded by a sniper firing from behind their line, and 2nd Lieut. Blenkinsop took over command till the arrival at night of Lieut. R.V. Hare. C.S.M. Lancaster of A Company was also badly wounded.

The men on the left of B Company, under Lieut. H.C.W. Haythornthwaite during these days, were in very close touch with the enemy, being separated from them in the same trench by a block about ten yards wide. They were the first of the Battalion to use rifle grenades, which were taken up to them by a party of the Buffs. On the night of the 28th April No. 6 Platoon was sent up to join the Company, but it was found that they could not be accommodated in the trench and they returned to Battalion Headquarters. All through this period the Company was existing under very difficult conditions. The evacuation of wounded was almost impossible, and Corpl. Hardy did excellent work in establishing an aid post and attending to wounded for four days and nights. He was subsequently mentioned in dispatches for this good work. Their only rations were taken up on the night of the 28th by a party of No. 9 Platoon under Corpl. Hall, and water was collected from shell holes in empty ammunition boxes.

Whilst in the front line, both A and B Companies were constantly under fire from trench mortars ("sausages") and snipers, some of whom were firing from the rear. Several of the posts held by B Company were blown in, and in one, occupied by Sergt. Bennison and ten men, all were hit except Ptes. Walters and Fenwick. In another post the shelter was blown in and several men wounded and buried. Pte. Robinson, the only man not hit, crossed the open to the next post, but was unable to obtain assistance. He thereupon went back, and under constant fire, dug out several men. For this action he was awarded the D.C.M. and Croix de Guerre.

The machine-gun section was in action on the 26th April, and for his good work in handling them Lieut. W.P. Gill was awarded the Military Cross. After being withdrawn on the night of the 26th the guns were kept in reserve at Battalion Headquarters.

During the whole of the four days the Battalion was in the line, parties from D Company under 2nd Lieut. G. Angus did good work in distributing rations, which were brought up from Poperinghe to Zonnebeke Crossing by limber. The exact location of the different parties was doubtful, and the absence of roads, tracks or landmarks made the delivery of rations to the men a very unpleasant task.

On the 30th April came news of relief. A Company were relieved at night by the 1st Battalion Northumberland Fusiliers and moved back to the Convent near Velorenhoek. B Company had further unpleasant experiences. Their relief by a Battalion of the Royal Fusiliers took place nearly at dawn, and it was impossible to get further than Hicks' Farm before it was too light to move. They were accordingly put into a barn and some trenches for the day, being still only about 300 yards from the enemy, whose aeroplanes were very active directing fire on to the position. This fire was fairly successful, and the barn was hit and set on fire and Lieut. A.B. Hare wounded. The men showed excellent discipline on this occasion and stood fast till led out to occupy a neighbouring trench. At night the Company rejoined the rest of the Battalion at the Convent, where the whole were accommodated in trenches near the road.

In addition to the honours already mentioned the following were subsequently awarded for work during this period:—Capt. T. Welch received the Military Cross for his work with B Company on Gravenstafel Ridge, being the first officer in the Brigade to win the decoration; R.S.M. G. Perry, who had been doing excellent work for the Battalion since mobilization, was granted the D.C.M. for his work in organising ration parties; and C.S.M.s McNair and Bousfield (afterwards commanding 15th D.L.I.) also received the D.C.M. for gallantry after casualties to officers. Others, who did excellent work, but received no decoration, were Lieut. W.F.E. Badcock, Signalling Officer, and his Sergeant, H. Elliott; Sergts. Linsley and Wallace, of B Company; Pte. Newton of A Company, and Pte. Hall of C Company.

The casualties had been fairly heavy, and included fifteen officers, amongst whom was Lieut.-Col. H.C. Watson, who left the Battalion sick on the 28th April. Capt. J.W. Jeffreys had assumed command with Lieut. R.V. Hare as Adjutant.

Second Phase.

On the 30th April the enemy delivered another attack, using gas. This fell mainly on the Irish Regiment, but the 6th Battalion in reserve occupied battle positions, and collected many men who were driven back by the gas. At night the Battalion marched back to huts in Brielen Wood, where it rested for 24 hours. Leaving there, it marched to St. Jansterbiezen, where it was inspected on the morning of the 2nd May by Sir John French, who thanked the men for their good work and praised especially A and B Companies. On the 8th May a draft of officers joined the Battalion, and the following day a move was made back to Brielen Woods. Here the Battalion, living in bivouacs, was in Divisional reserve for one day. The transport and Q.M. Stores moved into a field near Poperinghe.

After this short rest the Battalion learnt that it was to return to the scene of its first experiences. On the 10th May it marched to Potijze and occupied the G.H.Q. line near the railway and some dug-outs in the cutting south-east of Ypres. Here the men were shelled at intervals, particularly on the 13th, and spent the nights on working parties. It was whilst in this area that the new gas respirators, consisting of a pad of cotton wool and a strip of muslin, were issued on a scale of one to every twelve men. On the 19th May Major W.E. Taylor, York and Lancaster Regiment, arrived and took over command from Capt. Jeffreys. Two days later the Battalion was relieved by the East Surrey Regiment, and returned to Brielen huts.

During the next few days the artillery fire increased considerably on both sides, and just before dawn on Whit Monday, the 24th May, the Germans launched their gas attack. The gas cloud drifted towards Brielen and the men were roused and moved about half a mile from the camp to which they returned for breakfast and to prepare to move into action. The morning had turned out bright and fine when they paraded and marched off to Potijze. In those days the road leading out of Ypres eastwards was still marked by leafy trees, and as the Battalion marched along it, trees, branches and leaves were lying about, brought down by the heavy fire. Arriving at the wood, which was being heavily shelled, the men were put into ditches and half-dug trenches. Later in the day packs were collected, and in the lighter "Fighting Order" the men manned the G.H.Q. line in front of the wood, being in reserve to the 3rd Battalion Middlesex Regiment, who were under orders to deliver a counter-attack. Whilst taking up this position Major Taylor was wounded and 2nd Lieut. J.M. Hare killed, and Capt. Jeffreys again assumed command. The counter-attack was cancelled and the Battalion moved back to dug-outs on the Menin Road, where it stayed all the next day.

On the night of the 25th May the whole Battalion paraded as a working party to dig a front line trench to fill a gap caused by the German attack. The right of this trench was on the railway cutting, the enemy being on the other side of the cutting. The men worked magnificently and finished the task in less than two hours. As soon as it was completed the new trench was occupied by a Battalion of the Buffs. After two more nights spent on working parties the men were relieved and marched back to bivouacs in Brielen Wood. On the 2nd June orders were received to move further back, and they marched through Poperinghe to a field on the south of the town, where they spent the night and the next day, moving again on the 4th to bivouacs at Ouderdom.

The organisation of the Battalion was now to undergo a change which did not meet with universal approval amongst its members. On the 8th June it was amalgamated with the 8th Durham Light Infantry, the new Battalion being constituted as follows: Lieut.-Col. J. Turnbull, V.D. (8th D.L.I.) in command; Capt. G.A. Stevens (Royal Fusiliers), Adjutant; A Company (8th D.L.I.), Capt. T.A. Bradford; B Company (A and B Companies of 6th D.L.I.), Lieut. W.P. Gill; C Company (6th D.L.I.), Lieut. T.B. Heslop; D Company (6th D.L.I.), Capt. F.H. Livesay; Machine-gun section, 2nd Lieut. R.A. Howe (6th D.L.I.); transport section, Lieut. Ramsay (8th D.L.I.); Quartermaster, Lieut. W.M. Hope (6th D.L.I.). All supernumerary staff were sent to the base at Harfleur. At the same time the 7th Battalion became Divisional Pioneers and the 5th Battalion Loyal North Lancashire Regiment joined the 151st Brigade.

On the evening of the 11th June the new Battalion marched by Companies to dug-outs in the grounds of Kruisstraat Château, south of Ypres. The following day the march was resumed via the Lille gate and Maple Copse to Sanctuary Wood, where the Battalion was lent to the 149th Infantry Brigade to provide working parties for the improvement of the Hooge defences. It was during this move that the transport, on the 14th June, had its worst experience of the famous Hell Fire Corner, where it was shelled and a water cart was completely destroyed.

Wednesday, the 16th June, had been chosen for an attack on Hill 60 by the 3rd Division, the 50th Division being ordered to co-operate by making a demonstration. At 2.30 a.m. the Battalion moved into the support trenches, twenty minutes before the bombardment commenced. At 4.15 a.m. the 3rd Division assaulted, and their apparent success which could be seen from the rear was greeted with much enthusiasm by the men. About two hours later a message was received from a commanding officer in Zouave Wood that he was about to attack north-east of Hooge. Accordingly, two Companies under Major Hawdon were sent in support, the others being assembled ready to follow. The attack was cancelled, however, and at 7.30

a.m. the Battalion re-assembled in its original trenches. At night it moved up and relieved the 7th Northumberland Fusiliers in the Hooge defences. The disposition of Companies was as follows: B Company, under Lieut. Gill, were in "B9" trench. A Company, under Capt. Bradford, in "H13" and "H14" trenches; C Company, under Lieut. Heslop, in the Hooge Château stables; and D Company, under Capt. Livesay, in support in "H16" trench. The trenches, especially those occupied by B Company, had been much battered, and a considerable amount of work had to be done on them during the night. At this time the Château and stables were still standing, and though C Company were in occupation of the stables, the Germans held the Château, from the windows of which their snipers were able to give considerable trouble.

The following day was marked by considerable shelling, and at night a successful bombing enterprise was led against a sap head. For two days the position remained unchanged, the Battalion being engaged in repairing the trenches and carrying up rations and ammunition, till on the night of the 18th it was relieved by a Company of the 7th Northumberland Fusiliers and a Battalion of the Wiltshire Regiment, and went to F. hutments south of Vlamertinghe.

This concluded the Battalion's first tour in the "Salient."

CHAPTER II.
ARMENTIÈRES AND THE RETURN TO THE "SALIENT."

First Phase.

On Sunday, the 20th June, the Battalion marched off from Vlamertinghe at 8.30 a.m. through Ouderdom and Locre to Dranoutre, where it went into bivouacs at Corunna Farm, being now in the II Corps commanded by Sir Charles Ferguson, who inspected and addressed the men the following day. In the evening, after their inspection, they moved up to the front line and took over the trenches from "E1" to the barricade on the Kemmel-Wytschaete Road—a quiet sector except for trouble from snipers.

A few days after taking over, an interesting incident occurred. A notice board was put up in the German trenches bearing the words "Lemberg is taken." It was accompanied by cheering and the lighting of flares, to which the front line Companies replied by rapid fire in the direction of the board. The same day (23rd June) work was started on the mines, which were eventually blown up in the successful attack on the Wytschaete Ridge in June, 1917. Apart from this, nothing of interest occurred beyond the usual reliefs till the middle of July. An announcement which aroused considerable delight was made on the 15th July to the effect that leave to England was to be granted, two officers and three other ranks being allowed to be away at a time for periods of six and four days respectively.

On the 16th July the Battalion was relieved and moved from Kemmel at 7.30 p.m. proceeding via Dranoutre and Bailleul to Armentières, where it arrived at 1 a.m. the next morning and went into billets at the Blue factory. The following night it moved up to relieve Battalions of the Royal Scots and Monmouths. B Company under Lieut. R.V. Hare, took over "67" trench, C Company under Lieut. T.B. Heslop, "68" trench, A Company under Capt. Ritson (8th D.L.I.), "69" trench, and D Company under Capt. Livesay, Lille Post. The sector proved to be very quiet and the trenches exceptionally good. It is interesting to note that about this time the training of bombers was organised, and 2nd Lieut. P.H.B. Lyon of the Battalion was appointed first Brigade Bombing Officer.

The men were now beginning to realize that their first taste of conditions in France was not typical of the whole front, and that war had its more pleasant side. After the "Salient," the Armentières trenches were a picnic, and though there is little of historic interest to record concerning the tour, it formed the subject of many conversations and jests when harder times followed. Many times, probably, in the water-logged shell holes of Passchendaele in 1918 was it recalled how once at Armentières even the duck boards were cleaned daily and men were crimed for throwing matches on them. It is not forgotten either how the Battalion Band first came into being at Houplines.

On the 11th August, the 6th and 8th Battalions once more assumed a separate identity. Major Borrett, D.S.O., the King's Own, took over command of the 6th Battalion with Capt. Jeffreys once more as Adjutant. Four days later Major Borrett left and handed over the command to Capt. Jeffreys, 2nd Lieut. P.H.B. Lyon becoming Adjutant. On this re-organization the Companies of the Battalion became known as W, X, Y, and Z. About the same time the 5th Battalion Loyal North Lancashire Regiment left the Brigade, and was replaced by the 5th Battalion Border Regiment.

Early in September, some excitement was caused by the rumour that the "Mushroom," a circular trench in the Battalion sector, was mined and likely to be blown up. Bombers of W Company patrolled it and slept in it for six nights without result. On the 25th September the heavy firing at Loos caused a little anxiety. The day after this the Battalion sector was slightly altered by the taking over of the Houplines trenches from the 12th Division. A little more excitement than usual occurred on 13th October, when a demonstration was made by the artillery and the throwing of smoke bombs.

The tour ended on the 10th November, when the Battalion was relieved and marched to billets at La Creche, near Bailleul, where it stayed for a month enjoying its first rest since embarkation.

Second Phase.

Early in December it was known that the next tour was to be once more in the "Salient." On the 17th December the Battalion entrained at Steenwercke for Poperinghe, from where it marched to Dickebusch huts, which are always remembered as being built on islands in a sea of mud. The following night another march via Kruisstraat and Zillebeke brought the men to Maple Copse where they relieved the 11th Royal Scots (9th Division). The trenches were found to consist of holes and ditches which were worked on till they were quite good and dry. It was here that arrangements were first made for the prevention of trench feet.

Sunday, the 19th December, was marked by a German gas attack north of Hooge, but the Battalion was not involved. The following day the artillery activity continued, and Lieut.-Col. Jeffreys was wounded whilst going round a new piece of the line which had been taken over from the Argyll and Sutherland Highlanders. Major G.A. Stevens (8th D.L.I.) took over command, and the following day Capt. R.B. Bradford (afterwards Brig.-Gen. Bradford, V.C.) joined as Adjutant. An unusual occurrence took place on the 22nd December, when two Russians, who had been prisoners in Germany and had been working behind the line, escaped and came into the trenches in the Battalion sector. On Christmas Day the Battalion was out of the line and in the huts at Dickebusch. Capt. Bradford left on the 31st December to join the 7th Battalion, and was succeeded as Adjutant by 2nd Lieut. C.E. Yaldwyn.

On New Year's morning the Battalion had its first experience of a really heavy British bombardment of the enemy's trenches. The bombardment was so intense that it was possible to find one's way about Sanctuary Wood by the light of the gun flashes. The only other incident of importance in the first month of 1916 was the departure of the machine-gun section which, under 2nd Lieut. L. Brock, was sent to form part of the Brigade Machine Gun Company. To replace the guns, the first Lewis Guns were issued and put under the command of 2nd Lieut. J.P. Moffitt. It was also about this time that the Battalion journal, The Whizz-Bang, came into existence, edited and run by 2nd Lieut. Yaldwyn. Its illustrations by Lieut. Catford and articles were much appreciated, but, unfortunately, its publication ceased in November of the same year.

Throughout January and February there were local artillery combats which terminated with the capture of Hill 60 and "The Bluff." On the 1st March there was a demonstration at 5 p.m., which consisted of artillery and infantry fire and cheering as if for an attack. The following morning at 4.32 a.m. the 3rd Division attacked and captured International and New Year trenches and "The Bean" with over 200 prisoners. On the 18th March, the Battalion was relieved and moved to Poperinghe by train from Ypres. Four days later it returned again by train and took over the recently captured Bluff trenches from the 10th Royal Welsh Fusiliers (3rd Division). These trenches were round the edge of the Bluff crater and were in a very bad condition due to the rain and heavy shelling, and were littered with remnants of German equipment and their dead. X Company were on the right in New Year trench supported by Y Company in Gordon Post. W Company were in the centre in "The Loop," and Z Company on the left in "The Bean."

On the 27th March, at 4.15 a.m., the 3rd Division on the right attacked at St. Eloi, and during the attack the Medical Officer (Capt. White) and a party of stretcher bearers rendered valuable assistance. A few days later (2nd April) the Battalion was relieved by the Canadians, who had suffered heavily from shell fire in coming up, and moved again to Dickebusch, where there was a stay of two days before moving South to Scottish Lines at Westoutre and La Clyte.

A week later, on the 8th April, the Battalion was again in the line, this time relieving the 7th Battalion Shropshire Light Infantry in trenches N and O, in front of Wytschaete, with back area at La Clyte. These trenches were of the breastwork type. About this time there was a good deal of fighting on the left, where the Germans were trying to retake the St. Eloi craters.

On the 24th April the Battalion was relieved and marched to rest billets at Berthen. These billets were found to be farms scattered over a large area. A few days after arrival, Lieut.-Col. Jeffreys, D.S.O., returned and took over command from Lieut.-Col. Stevens, who went as Brigade Major to a Canadian Brigade. Early on the morning of the 30th the Battalion was roused by the news of a gas attack, but after standing to till daylight it was not required to move. A week later, 2nd Lieut. G. Kirkhouse was appointed Adjutant in place of 2nd Lieut. Yaldwyn, and on the 8th May the Battalion returned to La Clyte for four days working parties. The only other incidents of importance during May were an inspection by Sir Douglas Haig and the farewell inspection and address on the 16th by Brig.-Gen. Shea prior to his departure to take over command of the 30th Division. He was succeeded by Brig.-Gen. Westmorland.

On the 28th May the Battalion returned to the trenches it had left a month before, and on the 2nd June the men were able to watch the German attack between Hill 60 and Hooge and the Canadian counter-attacks on the following day. Lieut. Ebsworth, M.C., D.C.M., East Lancashire Regt., joined as Adjutant on the 7th June. During this tour the first Battalion raid was made by men of Y Company under 2nd Lieut. H.C. Annett and 2nd Lieut. J.F.G. Aubin, who was Battalion Bombing Officer. The party consisted of 24 men, including two bombing squads, and had as its object identification of the enemy on the immediate front. The night of the 6th June was chosen and the party went out as arranged. In No Man's Land they met a large enemy wiring party and their object was not attained. Three nights later, however, a German was captured, and again on the 12th the raiding party went out, this time with the object of killing Boches. They entered the enemy trench, and after doing considerable damage with bombs and rifles, returned without casualty.

Apart from these incidents the sector was on the whole quiet, except for a certain amount of sniping. The principal feature was the daily enemy bombardment with trench mortars, which lasted from one to three hours, and was on occasions very heavy. The front line, however, was thinly held and very few casualties resulted. After receiving two drafts of 190 and 110 men respectively the Battalion was relieved on 7th August by the 7th Battalion King's Own and moved to its old billets at Berthen.

This ended the second phase of its war history, and a few days later it moved South to the Somme area.

CHAPTER III.
THE SOMME.

First Phase.

On the 10th August, 1916, the Battalion entrained at Godewaersvelde, and detraining at Candas, marched to Heuzecourt and spent four days resting. The 15th, 16th and 17th were spent in marching through Vignacourt and Villers Bocage to Baizieux, where the men bivouaced in the wood. Here two accidents occurred. Major F. Walton, Second in Command, and Lieut. Ebsworth, M.C., Adjutant, were thrown from their horses and sustained broken limbs. 2nd Lieut. Kirkhouse resumed duties as Adjutant.

Nearly a month was spent in the wood, the time being devoted to training in the new wave formation for the coming offensive. It was about this time that distinguishing marks were adopted in the Division and the Battalion began to wear the red diamonds which came to be regarded with almost as much pride as the cap badge, and continued to be worn as long as the Battalion existed as a unit in France. On the 6th September Brig.-Gen. N.J.G. Cameron took over command of the Brigade. Four days later the Battalion moved to bivouacs in Becourt Wood, and there the final preparations were made for action, and amid the growing violence of the artillery preparation it moved again on the 14th September to Shelter Wood.

Zero for the second phase of the Somme battle was 6.20 a.m. on the 15th September. The 149th and 150th Infantry Brigades were then in the front line between High Wood and Martinpuich with the 151st Brigade in reserve. At zero the Battalion moved from Shelter Wood by way of Sausage Valley to an old German trench at the south-west corner of Mametz Wood. About noon a further forward move was made, Y and Z Companies to the northern edge of the wood, and W and X Companies to a position a little further forward between Mametz and Bazentin-le-Petit Woods. So far the Battalion had escaped shell fire, and the men were much interested in prisoners who were being escorted to the rear. About 11 a.m. a message was received that the 47th Division had failed to take High Wood, and that the two Brigades of the 50th Division had secured their objectives. Later came a message that the 47th Division had taken High Wood at the second attempt.

Rations arrived about 5 p.m., and whilst they were being distributed Lieut.-Col. Jeffreys returned from Brigade Headquarters with orders to move up at once. Accordingly the Battalion paraded and marched up the road to the

Quarry at Bazentin-le-Petit. By this time the area was full of movement. Guns, ammunition, ration wagons and troops were everywhere moving up after the advance.

After a conference at Brigade Headquarters orders were again issued for a move, and at 9 p.m. the Battalion in fours, led by the Commanding Officer and a guide from the Northumberland Fusiliers moved from the Quarry with orders to attack from Eye and Clarke's trenches at 9.30 p.m. The attack was to be made in four waves, with the 9th Durham Light Infantry, who had been in position all the afternoon, on the right, the 6th in the centre, and the 5th Border Regiment on the left. Unfortunately the guide lost his way, and after unnecessary wandering the head of the Battalion arrived in Clarke's trench, at the junction with Bethel sap, at 9.15 p.m. After considerable difficulty, owing to ignorance of the ground, the Companies got into position. W Company, under Capt. J. Cook, was on the left of the first wave, and X Company, under Capt. W.F.E. Badcock, on the right, with Z (left) and Y (right) in support. Just as they got into Clarke's trench 2nd Lieut. Annett, commanding Y Company, was killed, and 2nd Lieut. B.J. Harvey, though wounded, took command.

At the time appointed for the attack the 5th Border Regiment could not be located, so the 6th and 9th Durham Light Infantry, after waiting about an hour, advanced. Crossing Hook trench, which had been the enemy front line in the morning and was now held by remnants of the 149th Brigade, they moved down the slope towards Starfish and Prue trenches, the first objective. They were met by a certain amount of machine-gun and rifle fire, and had a few casualties, including Capt. Badcock, who was wounded. The 6th Battalion continued to advance, however, until completely checked by machine-gun fire, and then took cover in ditches and shell holes. It was then discovered that there was a considerable gap on the right, but by moving men in that direction touch was regained with the 9th Battalion.

About 3.30 a.m. on the 16th the Commanding Officer took up Z Company to reinforce the front line, and the 5th Border Regiment also moved up at the same time. The whole line was then pushed forward and straightened. Battalion Headquarters remained in Clarke's trench.

Further orders were received to attack again at 9.15 a.m., but they never readied the Companies, and nothing happened. Things were fairly quiet during the day, and at night a shallow communication trench was dug over the ridge and attempts made to improve the forward positions. Efforts were also made to collect the Battalion into Companies, but on the 17th the only parties under the control of Headquarters were half of W Company, under Capt. Cook, part of X Company, under Lieut. Harriss, a Platoon of Z Company, under Lieut. W.B. Hansell, and Y Company, in reserve in a sunken road, under 2nd Lieuts. McVicker and Richardson. It was known that other isolated groups were in positions in the front line. One of these was organised for defence under orders of Private B. McLinden of X Company, who subsequently received the Military Medal.

The chief obstacle to a further advance was an enemy strong point called the Crescent. Accordingly a party was organised to attack it, consisting of two bombing squads, one each from the 6th and 8th Battalions under 2nd Lieut. J.F.G. Aubin, now Brigade Bombing Officer. Leaving by way of Crescent Alley at 6 p.m., they met with considerable shell fire and were disorganised. Re-forming, however, they went out again with the same result. The shelling proved to be the preliminary to an attack on the 150th Brigade, which was beaten off, Y Company being used to assist their neighbours with Lewis guns.

The following day (18th) was misty, and it was thought that the Germans were evacuating Starfish trench. An attack was therefore ordered to occupy it. This attack was made by the 6th Battalion on the left and the 9th on the right, each providing 100 men. 2nd Lieut. W. Little, with 50 men of W Company, composed the Battalion's front line, and 2nd Lieut. W.F. Charlton, with 50 of Z Company, the supporting line. A few men of other Companies were also mixed with these two lines. Shortly after starting they came under heavy machine-gun fire and had a number of casualties, including 2nd Lieut. Charlton, who was killed. Some of the party returned to their line during the day and others at night. All who had been near the enemy trench reported it to be strongly held.

During the morning Y Company were sent up to relieve W, X and Z Companies in the front line. Owing to the trenches being very muddy after rain, and at all places very shallow, this was a difficult operation. To add to the difficulty the 8th Battalion began to arrive to relieve the Battalion before the Company relief was complete. However, they at last got out and moved back to 6th Avenue East and the intermediate line, where two days were spent in cleaning up. Here Lieut. Ebsworth rejoined as Adjutant, and the officers and men who had been left at the transport lines also came up.

On the 20th September, the Battalion moved further back to shelter in Mametz Wood, where a draft of 50 men from the 2/6th Battalion, Essex Regiment, joined. After four days' rest it again went forward to the intermediate line. The same day Major Wilkinson, of the 149th Machine Gun Company, joined as second in command. The following night the whole Battalion turned out to dig a jumping-off trench. Lieut.-Col. Jeffreys took them as far as the Battalion Headquarters of the 5th Durham Light Infantry from where Lieut. Ebsworth and a guide led them to the position.

The guide lost his way, and after wandering about nearly all night, the Battalion returned without doing any work.

On the 26th September Lieut.-Col. Jeffreys left the Battalion to proceed to England for three months' rest, and Major Wilkinson took over command. The following day a move was made to Hook trench, where the men lived in small shelters and provided working parties at nights. This trench was on the sky line, and as a result received considerable attention from the enemy gunners. To prevent casualties, and also to provide more room, two Companies were pushed forward on the 28th to Starfish trench. From these positions, in the afternoon, the Battalion relieved the 9th Battalion in the front line. The relief was observed, and the communication trench shelled. The disposition of Companies was, from right to left: Y, Z, W, X, each Company having two Platoons in the front line (North Durham Street) and two Platoons in the support line (South Durham Street). At night they occupied battle positions, and extended the trench they occupied by 150 to 300 yards. The 9th Battalion was in support in Crescent Alley. On the left were the 5th Border Regiment, and on the right the 47th Division, but it was not possible to get into touch with the flanks during the night. The Company Commanders were now W Company, 2nd Lieut. Barnett; X Company, 2nd Lieut. Lean; Y Company, Lieut. Catford; and Z Company, Capt. Peberdy. By dawn all preparations, including the alteration of watches to winter time, were completed for the attack, which had been ordered for the 1st October.

The preliminary bombardment commenced at 7 a.m. and continued till zero (3.15 p.m.), when it changed to a barrage. Unfortunately there were some casualties from shells falling short, the total casualties for the day being about 40, including the Commanding Officer wounded. Lieut.-Col. R.B. Bradford, now commanding the 9th Battalion, asked for and was given permission to take command of the two Battalions, and for his subsequent work that day was awarded the V.C. He arrived at Battalion Headquarters at zero, and at once went up to the front line.

The attack commenced at 3.15 p.m., but, partly on account of the failure of the 47th Division on the right, and partly owing to the wire not being properly cut, the attackers were held up by machine-gun fire and suffered heavy casualties. After considerable fighting with bombs and rifles three Lewis gun teams of X Company, under 2nd Lieut. T. Little and 2nd Lieut. C.L. Tyerman, and one team of W Company under 2nd Lieut. Barnett, succeeded in getting a footing in the first objective. These organised the position and carried on bombing attacks, 2nd Lieut. Little being killed. During these operations Lieut.-Col. Bradford arrived on the scene, and immediately took charge of the situation, and under his direction and leadership the whole of the first objective was gained. A Company of the

9th Battalion then came up, and using the new position as a starting point, advanced and took the final objective after dark.

About dusk a counter-attack was attempted by the enemy on the right front. Advancing in extended order, about twenty of the enemy were challenged, and they all cheered, shouting "Hooray." As they showed no further friendly signs they were fired on and driven off. During the night a further counter-attack developed from the valley on the right, but this also was repulsed.

The following day, by organised bombing, the whole of the final objective was captured and held, and communication trenches were dug back to North Durham Street.

The casualties during the two days had been very heavy, and included amongst the officers, in addition to those already mentioned, 2nd Lieut. Peacock, killed, and 2nd Lieut. Lean, Capt. Peberdy, Lieut. Cotching, 2nd Lieut. Barnett and 2nd Lieut. Appleby wounded. Amongst the decorations gained were Military Medals awarded to Corporal Dixon and Privates Rushforth and Atkinson, all signallers, and Private Turnbull of Y Company. Good work was also done by Sergeants Gowland and Winslow.

On the night of the 2nd October Lieut.-Col. Bradford handed over the command of the Battalion to Lieut. Ebsworth, and it was relieved by the 7th Northumberland Fusiliers the night after. Owing to the mud the relief did not commence until 4 a.m., and it was almost dawn before the Battalion reached Headquarters, from where it was led by Lieut. Ebsworth to Starfish trench. Here it was joined by R.S.M. Perry and the C.S.M.'s and a draft which had been used as a carrying party. The officers left were Lieut. Ebsworth, 2nd Lieut. Kirkhouse, Adjutant; 2nd Lieut. K.B. Stuart, Signalling Officer, and 2nd Lieut. Tyerman; the Medical Officer, Capt. J.G. Hill, arrived later.

After a short rest the Battalion marched back to bivouacs in Becourt Wood for one night.

Second Phase.

On the 4th October, the Battalion moved back to tents in Henencourt Wood, where drafts arrived, and remained for three weeks, reorganising and training. The Company Commanders were now:—W Company, 2nd Lieut. A.S. Tate; X Company, 2nd Lieut. J.H.F. Ludgate; Y Company, 2nd Lieut. R.H. Stewart; and Z Company, 2nd Lieut. C.L. Tyerman.

At the end of this period, on the 23rd October, the Battalion left the Wood and marched back to Becourt, where two days were spent in tents. On the 25th October the men were on the move again over familiar ground and soon found themselves in tents just outside Mametz Wood. After a week spent on working parties they moved up to the front line, W Company, now under 2nd Lieut. R.H. Wharrier, being in front in Snag trench and the other three Companies in close support in the Flers line. On the night of Saturday, the 4th November, X, Y and Z Companies took over the front line in preparation for an attack on the Butte de Warlencourt on the Sunday morning. Zero had been fixed for 9.15 a.m. and the relief was not complete, owing to the extremely bad state of the trenches, till 9 a.m. The Battalion was disposed for the attack with X Company on the right, Y in the centre, Z on the left and W in support, with the 9th Battalion on the left flank and the 8th on the right. This fateful day, 5th November, proved to be the most disastrous the Battalion had yet passed through. The enemy position was exceptionally strong, the trenches from which the attack started were so muddy that several men were drowned in them, and the time for preparation was so short that the attack broke down almost as soon as it had started. The casualties were very heavy, and included amongst the officers 2nd Lieut. K.B. Stuart, 2nd Lieut. Fell, 2nd Lieut. A.S. Ritson, 2nd Lieut. S. Robson, 2nd Lieut. T.F. Applegarth, and 2nd Lieut. G.W. Robson, all killed, and all the remaining Company officers, except 2nd Lieut. Wharrier, wounded. Amongst the honours awarded were the M.C. to 2nd Lieut. Wharrier and the Military Medal to L.-Cpl. H. Cruddace, who was also promoted to be sergeant. A monument was afterwards erected on the Butte to the memory of those of the Battalion who fell on this day.

On the following night the Battalion was relieved by the 5th Battalion and went back to Mametz Wood, where it stayed till the end of the month supplying working parties daily. Several new officers joined here, including Lieut.-Col. H.M. Allen, Black Watch, who took over command; Lieut. (now Major) Ebsworth becoming Second in Command.

Towards the end of the month came rumours of a rest, and on the 30th the Battalion marched off once more to Becourt, where it was this time accommodated in huts. After a night there it marched back to billets at Warloy, where it stayed during the whole of December, training and resting. The rest was thoroughly enjoyed by all ranks. On Christmas Day sports were held which included a mounted officers' race won by Lieut. H.T. Bircham, M.C., transport officer.On New Year's Day the Battalion was on its way back to the line. The first day's march took it to billets in Albert, the billets being partially destroyed houses. The following day the march was resumed to a hut camp near the quarry at Bazentin-le-Petit, well known to the few remaining survivors of the 15th September. After a few days in this camp, troubled only by an occasional shell, a move was made into High Wood West camp, a cheerless place consisting of black tarpaulin huts.

From this and a similar camp across the valley (High Wood East) the Battalion did two tours in the front line at Factory Corner, where the line consisted of more or less isolated posts. The support line, where a few days were spent, was just in front of Flers. During these tours the weather was exceedingly cold and the men suffered considerably, both in the line and in the camp. There was also a considerable amount of shell fire. Parties carrying up rations and pushing trolleys up the light railway from Clarke's Dump had several casualties, and on one occasion the camp was hit and all the signallers who had been left out of the line for training became casualties. In the line itself the only outstanding incident happened to a patrol which found itself surrounded one night, but succeeded in getting back safely. Towards the end of the month came rumours of relief, and on the 24th January the Division was relieved by the 1st Australian Division. The Battalion came out to a new hut camp on the Beaver Road, between the Bazentin and Mametz Woods. The next day it marched to Becourt Camp, the air being full of rumours as to the future.

It soon became known, however, that the Division was moving south to take over a section of the line hitherto held by the French, still in the Somme area, just south of Peronne. From Becourt the Battalion continued its march to Ribemont. The march was uneventful except for the fact that the two rear Companies took a wrong turning, and after a roundabout journey arrived late at the halting place for dinner. At Ribemont it stayed for about three weeks, during which training was carried out, the men being accommodated in barns. Col. Allen was still in command with Lieut. T.J. Arnott (Gordon Highlanders) as Adjutant. There was little of interest during this period and, on the whole, everybody was pleased when the move was resumed to huts at Hamel. After a few days there the Battalion marched to billets at Proyart, where Lieut.-Col. J.W. Jeffreys, D.S.O., returned and took over command. Again, in three or four days it marched to Foucaucourt, where it was in Divisional Reserve. This village, which had at one time been in the front line system, was practically nothing but ruins and the Battalion was accommodated in a large camp of French huts, fitted with wire beds, each hut holding about 150 men. Here, final preparations were made for the line, which was visited by officers who reported that the trenches were dry and in good condition. It was very frosty weather at this time, but unfortunately before the Battalion moved up a thaw had set in. The relief of the 5th Yorkshire Regiment will never be forgotten by those of the Battalion who took part in it. Following on the methods adopted by the French the relief took place through very long communication trenches, running from Estrées through Berny to the line in front of Misery. These trenches, as a result of the thaw, were everywhere knee deep in mud and usually waist deep, and men arrived in the line without boots and in a few cases without trousers, having lost them in the mud. The experiences of X

Company were perhaps the worst. Leaving camp at about 5 p.m., then 130 strong, they were met by guides, who lost their way, and eventually arrived in the front line at dawn, having lost over 100 men stuck in the mud. The relief was not reported complete till 4 p.m. the next day. The front line trenches were worse if possible than the communication trenches, and the days that followed were most unpleasant. There was very little cover from enemy snipers, who were pretty active, and there were several casualties from fishtail trench mortars. One night was marked by a very intense "strafe" for a short time with rifle grenades and trench mortars. It afterwards appeared that this was the enemy's parting shot, for soon after the Division was relieved the enemy's extensive retirement on this sector took place. After two tours in the front line, one in support in trenches round Berny, and one in reserve at Foucaucourt, the Battalion was relieved early in March by the 2/5th South Staffordshire Regiment (59th Division), who had just come from Ireland and had not previously seen any fighting in France. On relief the Battalion returned to Foucaucourt. Towards the end of the tour Lieut.-Col. Jeffreys left the Battalion for a few days in hospital, during which time Major Little, of the 5th Border Regiment, and Major Crouch of the 9th Durham Light Infantry, both held command. He returned, however, when the Battalion came out of the line. This ended the tour in the Somme region, but the Battalion did not leave the area till the end of the month, the period being spent in huts at Morcourt, where an energetic programme of training and sports was carried out. The principal feature of the sports was the success of members of the Battalion, including Sergt. Young and Ptes. Nimney and Moody in the Brigade and Divisional boxing contests. Although there were no outstanding incidents to record of this training, Morcourt seems to mark one of those turning points in the history of the Battalion from which all subsequent events date. So many small things occurred there that it was remarked by later comers that it appeared to them that the Morcourt training must have lasted for months. One event, however, can be pointed to as a turning point. On the 25th March, Lieut.-Col. Jeffreys, who had never fully recovered from the wounds received in Sanctuary Wood, was ordered to return to England on account of ill-health, and handed over command to Major W.D. Carswell Hunt, M.C., of the 7th Durham Light Infantry. Colonel Jeffreys' personal influence and fighting qualities, strongly reflected even in his absence in those officers who had received their early training under him, had been largely responsible for the reputation and the success of the Battalion during its first two years of fighting and his departure was greatly regretted by all ranks.

A few days after he left, the Battalion was on the move to take part in the battle which was about to begin at Arras.

CHAPTER IV.
ARRAS.

First Phase.

From Morcourt the Battalion moved by motor 'buses through Amiens to Talmas preparatory to a long trek on foot. The first two nights were spent at Wargnies and Havernas. Here a famous Church Parade was held, at which the Commanding Officer, in the absence of a Chaplain, preached his first and, as it proved, his last sermon. From there the Battalion marched to Longuevillette and then to Vacquerie-le-Bourcq, spending a night at each place. About this time Lieut. Arnott left the Battalion and Lieut. G.D.R. Dobson (7th Durham Light Infantry) became Adjutant. The next day Blangerval and Blangermont were reached and a short stay made, half the Battalion being accommodated in each village. From here Major Hunt went up by car to see the forward area and died of heart failure on the journey. He was brought back to St. Pol, where he was buried in the cemetery, representatives of several battalions forming the funeral procession. Major A. Ebsworth, M.C., took over command.

When the march was resumed the direction was changed, and, moving eastwards, billets were reached at Neuville-au-Cornet. Rumours were now spreading of the forthcoming battle and a further march to Villers-sur-Simon left no doubt that the Battalion would be involved. These were the last billets occupied by the men, the next portion of the trek bringing them to huts at Montenescourt, about six miles due west of Arras. Here Lieut.-Col. F.W. Robson, D.S.O. (5th Yorkshire Regiment) arrived to take over the command, which he held for nearly a year.

On the evening of the 11th April, in a blinding snowstorm, the Battalion moved forward to the fight. Marching through Arras, they came to the caves at Ronville. These caves were like nothing seen before. Excavated by Spanish prisoners in the middle ages to provide stone for the building of the city, they extended over an enormous area, and were capable of holding thousands of men. The sensation of finding oneself in this huge underground town, complete with electric light and water supply, after stumbling down a long, uneven stairway, will not be forgotten by those who survive.

After one night here, the caves had to be evacuated next morning to make room for more troops coming up. The Germans had now been driven back as far as Wancourt, which was captured the previous day. On leaving the caves, cellars in Ronville village were occupied. No sooner were the men in, however, than orders were received to move further forward. The Battalion paraded on the road leading to Beaurains, which was crowded with vehicles and men, and marched off in the afternoon. After their experiences of trench warfare the sight of open, rolling country, the scene of yesterday's fighting, was very strange and, to some, invigorating. Passing through the ruins of Beaurains and Neuville Vitasse, the route turned across country towards Wancourt, and about dusk the Battalion reached a sunken road, where it halted. Owing to a delay in the arrival of the Lewis gun limbers, the Lewis gunners were behind the rest of the Battalion, and some difficulty was experienced by them in locating the sunken road. Up to this point there had been no firing or signs of activity. After a conference of Commanding Officers a relief of the 14th Division was arranged. W, X and Y Companies moved a little further up and occupied Niger and Nepal trenches, which were some distance behind the front line, and Z Company were sent to dig a trench a little further forward near Wancourt cemetery. Here they remained for the day. At night detailed orders were received for an attack at dawn, the Battalion's frontage being near Wancourt Tower.

At 1 a.m. on the 14th April the men moved to the assembly position in the dry bed of the Cojeul River, with the 8th Battalion in support and 5th Border Regiment in reserve, the 9th Battalion being already in a line just south of Guemappe. The original orders had now been considerably altered, and zero hour arrived before fresh orders had been circulated to the Companies. The result was that at 4.30 a.m., after moving in file from the assembly position to a bank, some 200 yards in front, the Battalion advanced under a barrage in four waves of Companies, W being front and Z in rear, with no orders except a rough indication of the direction.

As they advanced they were met by very heavy machine-gun fire from the front and from Guemappe in their left rear. W and X Companies reached the ridge 500 yards from the starting point, and passing down the other side, were not seen again during the day. Y and Z Companies also reached the ridge, but could get no further. Later they were joined by the 8th Battalion, which was also held up.

The fighting then died down, but apart from one brief message from X Company no trace could be found of the two front Companies, and the casualties in the remaining two were very heavy. To add to the confusion, the 56th Division on the right had lost direction, and men of the London Regiment were everywhere mixed with those of the 50th Division.

At dusk orders were received that the line on the ridge would be taken over by the London Rifle Brigade. As soon as the light permitted search was made for W and X Companies. Eventually the remnants consisting of 4 officers and about 20 men were discovered. Having reached a small system of trenches, they had organised their defence and successfully beaten off determined attempts to surround them. About 80 men were finally assembled after the relief, and more joined the Battalion during the next few days, but the casualties amounted to over 200, or more than 50 per cent, of the total fighting strength. The officers killed were Capt. Brock, Lieut. Richardson, and 2nd Lieuts. Greener, Payne and Newton, whilst many were wounded. Capts. R.S. Johnson and H. Walton, commanding W and X Companies, were subsequently awarded the Military Cross, and Corporal Betts the D.C.M. and Croix de Guerre.

After burying as many bodies as could be recovered, the remnants of the Battalion moved back to dug-outs in the Hindenburg Line on Telegraph Hill, which were reached, after a roundabout march, at dawn.

From these dug-outs the Battalion returned next day to the caves at Ronville, where it was re-organised and re-equipped ready for further action. After four days' rest it again moved up, on the 21st April, this time to dug-outs in the trench system known as "The Harp," the Q.M. Stores remaining in Arras, where on the 22nd April Lieut. Lewis, acting Q.M., was killed by a shell. In "The Harp" fighting stores were issued, as the Battalion was to be in reserve for the attack on the 23rd April. At zero hour, just at dawn on that date, St. George's Day, the bombardment commenced, and the sight of the gun flashes against the red sky as the Battalion moved forward will not readily be forgotten. After two halts in sunken roads orders were received to occupy Niger trench once more, but by this time the fighting had died down. Although constantly on the alert, no further orders were received, and after two nights there, the Battalion was relieved by the 14th Division and returned to Telegraph Hill. One night was spent there, and the following day, the 27th, it entrained at Arras for Mondicourt, from where it marched to billets at Humbercourt, arriving about 3 a.m.

Here a few days were spent resting and training, and on the 1st May a march was ordered to Berles-au-Bois, which was found to be a village of ruins without inhabitants. After one night there the Battalion marched to Riviere-Grosville, where the billets were quite good. Here Lieut. G.D.R. Dobson went to hospital, and Lieut. R.B. Ainsworth became Adjutant. Two or three days were spent there, and on the 3rd May a return was made to Humbercourt. Here very pleasant days were spent in training, particularly those on the range at Lucheux Forest, where elaborate field firing schemes were carried out.

After about a fortnight there the Battalion was ordered up in reserve for an attack by the 33rd Division and marched to Monchy-au-Bois, where the accommodation was found to consist of an open field in which was a trench line and much wire. Shelters were erected of ground sheets, and a few tents obtained, and in these the men lived for five days, training being continued. Their services were not required in the line, however, and they marched back to Laherliere. Here a long stay was expected, but the following day the journey was resumed to Souastre, where the Battalion spent perhaps the most enjoyable month in its history. The men were accommodated in a hut camp built round a large parade and sports ground. As a result of easy training, plenty of recreation and fine weather, the moral of the men reached a very high level.

Second Phase.

On the 15th June the Battalion returned to hold the line which it had helped to gain in April. Leaving Souastre, it marched to support at a camp near Henin-sur-Cojeul. There was practically no accommodation here and ground sheets had to be used as shelters. The following day it relieved the 10th Battalion Essex Regiment in the front line, just south of the Cojeul River Valley, opposite Cherisy. After four days in this sector it went out to Divisional reserve near Boisleux-au-Mont, where, on the 27th June, it was visited by Col. the Hon. W.L. Vane, the Honorary Colonel of the Battalion. A regular system of reliefs, which lasted for three months, now commenced. Under this system the Battalion had two periods of four days in the front line and one in support at Henin or Neuville Vitasse, followed by eight days in reserve in camp near Mercatel. The weather was good on the whole, and the trenches in excellent condition. The enemy was only moderately active and there were very few casualties. One of the Battalion areas in this sector was the bank from which the attack started on the 14th April, and whilst there a cross was erected to the memory of those who fell on that day.

As a result of their long stay here, the men became very familiar with the whole area, and their experiences in the communication trenches, Foster Avenue, Shikar Lane, Kestrel Avenue, Avenue Trench and others were talked of for long after. Neither did they forget Lone Sap, from which the enemy captured two of their comrades, Cable Trench, which was raided by a party under 2nd Lieut. B.R. Leatherbarrow, Concrete Trench, the Hindenburg Line, the caves in Marliere Village, which on one occasion produced some interesting souvenirs left by the Boches, and many other localities.

Apart from minor raids and counter-raids, the only outstanding incident was the double raid of the 15th September. This operation was carried out by the 9th Durham Light Infantry in the afternoon and repeated by the 8th Durham Light Infantry in the evening. The Battalion was holding the sector immediately on the right of the raiders, and its function was to draw the enemy's attention and fire by the exhibition of dummy figures and a dummy tank, which were later on view at the United Services Museum in Whitehall. 2nd Lieut. Leatherbarrow was in charge of these dummies, assisted by Sergeant P. Finn, who was awarded the Military Medal for his work.

Other decorations earned during this period were Military Medals awarded to Corporal Nesbitt and Private Allison of X Company for digging out a man buried by shell fire, under very dangerous conditions.

Apart from good work in the line not only in patrolling, etc., but also in improving the trenches till they were probably as good as any on the whole front, considerable work was done on the erection of reserve camps and horse standings. It was with some regret therefore that when at Northumberland Lines, a very comfortable hut camp near Mercatel, the men heard that they were to leave the area before the winter.

Early in October they marched to a canvas camp at Gomiecourt, just off the main Bapaume road, and stayed there a short time training. The arrival of representatives from Divisions in the "Salient," to instruct in the methods adopted in the recent successful fighting there, left no doubts as to the next move.

CHAPTER V.
RETURN TO THE "SALIENT."

About the end of October the Battalion marched one night to Bapaume, where it entrained for Esquelbecq, north-west of Cassel. On detraining it marched to billets at Eringhem for two nights. From there the march was continued to Arneke, and there the men were told that a short stay would be made, but early the next day orders were received to march to Proven, just inside the Belgian frontier. On the road, however, fresh orders were received, and the latter part of the journey, from Wormhoudt, was done by train.

On arrival at Proven the Battalion occupied Piddington Camp on the Poperinghe road, and incidentally, renewed the acquaintance of Belgian mud. After one night there it moved for the next night to bivouacs known as Sarawak Camp, in the woods north of Poperinghe. This will probably be remembered as one of the dirtiest camps ever occupied. The last stage of the journey eastwards was done by train from Proven to Boesinghe. Arriving at the latter place in the morning, the men proceeded to Hulls Farm Camp close by, on the Ypres road. This camp was occupied, however, by the 4th Battalion Northumberland Fusiliers, which was moving up in the afternoon to take part in an attack along the Ypres-Staden railway north of Poelcapelle. Whilst lying in an open field waiting to occupy the camp a visit was received from a squadron of Gotha bombing planes, and about 20 casualties were suffered. About 5 p.m. the camp was taken over. Here the Battalion remained for three days, and had considerable experience of Hun aeroplane bombs, fortunately without further casualties. Exceptionally large working parties were demanded on each of the three nights, and their experiences were perhaps worse than those of the tour in the line which was to follow.

The third battle of Ypres was still in progress at this time, and Passchendaele had not yet been taken. On the front between the railway and Houthulst Forest, due north of Poelcapelle, the 149th Infantry Brigade had attacked and advanced the line slightly. A further attack by battalions of the 150th Brigade had partially failed, and about the beginning of November the battalion moved up to occupy the left sector of the line which was just inside the forest.

The journey up to the front line was far from pleasant. After crossing the canal it consisted of a six-mile walk along a duck-board track across one of the most devastated areas on the whole front, and to add to the difficulties, the enemy's artillery was very active. Owing to lack of roads for the transport, each man carried four days' rations. The position consisted of a series of water-logged shell holes, which were troubled considerably by low-flying aeroplanes. Battalion headquarters were in a pill-box known as Egypt House, which received very assiduous attention from the Boche gunners.

As it had been decided to make no further attack on this sector, though an improved position was desired, the nights were spent in pushing forward the posts as far as possible under cover of darkness. This was done very successfully, and the battalion line was advanced during the tour by 200 yards with very few casualties. Several decorations were obtained for this work including the Bar to the Military Cross to Capt. J.F.G. Aubin, M.C., commanding Y Company; and the Military Cross to Capt. P.H.B. Lyon, commanding X Company. Sergts. Britton and Cruddace were awarded Bars to the Military Medal.

After four days in the line, orders were received to move back to the neighbourhood of the canal for two days and then return. In view of the dangerous nature of reliefs, however, an alteration was asked for and obtained, and the Battalion completed its tour of six days. On relief by the 9th Battalion, it moved to Marsouin Farm Camp, near Pilkem, and spent a very unpleasant morning under fire from high velocity shells. Fortunately there were no casualties, and in the afternoon after the relief it again moved to a camp at Elverdinghe for a few nights.

From there it entrained to Watten, and marched to billets at Houlle. Here a very enjoyable month was spent. The maltery, where W and X Companies were billeted, was one of the best billets they had been in for some time. The great feature of this month's training was the sports. After winning the Brigade Football and Cross Country Cups, the battalion won a great triumph by obtaining the Divisional Cross Country Shield. This was given to the unit which had the largest proportion of its ration strength over the course in a certain time. The percentage obtained, 64 per cent., reflected the high state of efficiency to which the Battalion had now attained. For this high standard, a large amount of credit was due to R.S.M. G. Perry, D.C.M., who was unfortunately compelled by ill-health to leave the Battalion at Houlle, and subsequently went home, after nearly three years' active service. At his best on the parade ground and in his lectures on the history of his Regiment, his influence continued to be felt long after his departure, especially as he was succeeded by one whom he had trained in soldiering, C.S.M. J. Taylor, of X Company.

During the first week in December the visit of officers to the line disclosed the new sector to be taken over, which included Passchendaele village, recently captured by the Canadians. A few days later the Battalion entrained at Watten for Brandhoek, where it spent a short time in a hut camp in Divisional reserve. From there it marched up through Ypres to a camp just west of Potijze Wood, the scene of its first action in April, 1915. After two days there a further move was made to the forward area, into a number of shelters known as the Seine area. The next step was to the front line, which consisted of a series of shell hole positions on the Passchendaele Ridge. Not only were these uncomfortably wet, but they were very difficult to locate in the dark, and many will remember the trouble experienced in selecting the routes from the heap of debris of what had once been the village church. Battalion Headquarters were in a German pill-box known as Hamburg. Four days were spent in the front line, and the Battalion then went to Divisional reserve again at Brandhoek. After another tour in the line, it again moved to Brandhoek on Christmas Day, and there completed the 24 days which entitled it to a similar period of rest and training. The whole tour had been without any exciting incidents, and casualties were small, in spite of persistent shelling which made the duck-board tracks (H, K, R.A.M.C., tracks, etc.) very unpleasant. The Christmas at Brandhoek was thoroughly enjoyed by the men. On Boxing Day a Christmas dinner was provided, consisting of turkeys, puddings, port wine, beer, etc., the orderly work being done by the N.C.O.'s, and the carving by the officers. A visit was paid to the Battalion here by the Corps Commander (Lieut-Gen. Sir Aylmer Hunter-Weston), who congratulated the men on their appearance and bearing immediately after an uncomfortable trench tour.

From Brandhoek the Battalion moved by 'bus to the Steenvoorde area, where it was accommodated in very scattered billets for about ten days, during which it was training and resting. It then entrained at Eecke for Wizernes, near St. Omer, and marched to billets at Acquin. A stay of about a fortnight there was occupied in the use of an exceptionally good training area. A return was then made to the former front line, and detraining again at Brandhoek, the Battalion went this time to another hut camp known as Toronto. A similar system of reliefs as before was carried out and the tour was divided up into short periods at Brandhoek, St. Jean, and the Passchendaele sector. The line was somewhat quieter than on the previous occasion. The route to and from the trenches was now a new track called Judah track, a stretch of about three miles, which reflected great credit on the Pioneer Battalions. From Brandhoek to St. Jean and the return journeys were usually done by 'bus or light railway. The tour ended with a night in the cellars in the town of Ypres, and from there the Battalion marched to Ypres station and entrained to Wizernes again, and so to billets in St. Martin-au-Laert, a suburb of St. Omer. These billets were very good, and the advantage of being near a town was fully appreciated. The story of the Battalion would not be complete without a reference to the band, which, under the direction of Sergt. T.O. Hann, M.M., had reached a very high standard, and was second to none in the Division. With the buglers, whose smart appearance attracted much attention, a selection of music was played in the town daily at "Retreat." At this time, also, the Battalion concert party, the "Red Diamonds," trained by Capt. Cardew and Capt. Lyon, provided several very good entertainments.

It was now March, and the great enemy offensive on the Somme was expected. After three weeks, the rest was abruptly terminated by orders to entrain for Amiens, and about the second week in March the Battalion marched off from St. Martin, and entrained at Arques. At this time it was perhaps as efficient as any on the Western front, having had few casualties during the past year, and also having had a large proportion of rest and training. The officers knew their men both in and out of the line, and it was confidently expected that in the coming active operations great credit would be earned—but the overwhelming disasters of the next three months were never anticipated.

CHAPTER VI.
THE SOMME, THE LYS AND THE AISNE.

First Phase.

On detraining at Longeau, the Battalion marched to billets in Corbie, where it stayed for one night. The following day it moved to the south of the main Amiens-Peronne road to Marcelcave, and was then in Fifth Army Reserve. Here, for about a fortnight the finishing touches were put to the training. Included in the programme were the final stages of the Army Rifle Association competition, in which No. 6 Platoon were defeated by a Platoon of the 8th Durham Light Infantry in the final of the Brigade contest. The officers were taken up to certain areas near Peronne, where the Battalion might have to deliver counter-attacks in the event of a German success. About the middle of March rumours of the impending attack became more numerous, and the intelligence reports containing prisoners' statements, etc., were not reassuring. At last, the date of the attack, the 21st March, became fairly certain, and the drum fire heard in the distance on that day was not unexpected.

Orders were issued during the morning for a "stand-to" in readiness to move at very short notice, and about 3.45 p.m. instructions were received to entrain at Gouzeaucourt. In less than an hour the Battalion was on the march, the transport moving at the same time by road. After a short journey it detrained in the pitch dark at Brie, where Lewis guns, etc., were placed on lorries, the orders being to move into billets near Peronne. Whilst waiting for guides, however, a staff officer of the Division arrived with fresh orders. Instead of proceeding to billets the Battalion was to move straight into the fight. The Lewis guns were removed from the lorries and replaced by blankets, and the Battalion marched off in the direction of Tincourt. Just to the south of that village and in front of Beuzy a reserve system of partially dug trenches, known as the Green Line, was at once occupied. This line was the next defence system behind the Brown Line, where the 66th and other Divisions had been overwhelmed in the morning. On the morning of the 22nd March the men watched with interest tanks moving up to counter-attack, but on the whole things were quiet. In the afternoon the shelling became heavier, and in the distance large massed bodies of the enemy could be seen. The first contact occurred when a German scout was wounded and captured by a patrol. Orders were then received that the line was to be held at all costs. The apparent strength of the position, however, inspired confidence, and it was not till towards dusk that the first serious casualties occurred.

About 9 p.m. further orders were received to withdraw to a ridge in the rear, in front of Cardigny. The movement was successfully carried out in the dark, and at dawn the new position was reconnoitred and the dispositions completed. At 7 a.m. the startling orders were received that the Fifth Army was about to withdraw to the west of the Somme, and detailed instructions as to the rearguard action were issued. The Battalion was to cover the retirement of the 5th Durham Light Infantry, which would in turn cover a further withdrawal. Accordingly the village of Cardigny was occupied with a view to a temporary stand. No sooner was this done than the enemy were on the outskirts and their snipers and machine guns were giving considerable trouble. The position soon became untenable, and permission was obtained to withdraw. This was done without loss, largely owing to the courage of Y Company, who, under Capt. J.F.G. Aubin, M.C., formed the rearguard to the Battalion.

The next line of defence was a trench system on a ridge near Le Mesnil, which overlooked the Somme to the rear. Here things were quiet, though it was known that the enemy was working round the flanks, through Peronne on the left and Le Mesnil on the right. There was still a considerable amount of transport on the east of the river, and it was expected that a fight would follow to allow this to get away. After about two hours, however, orders came to cross the river by the Eterpigny footbridge. A route was taken across country towards this bridge, but there being no gap through the marshes and undergrowth, the Battalion was forced to turn aside through Le Mesnil village and, incidentally, to pass under a light shrapnel barrage. It was not known that the village was in the enemy's hands, but as soon as Z Company, who were leading, had reached the far side, the remaining Companies were attacked. Again Y Company distinguished itself, as did W and X Companies. They at once deployed, and though driven towards the marshes, successfully checked the enemy and eventually followed Z Company over the partially destroyed footbridge, about 300 yards long, with the loss of only two officers, Lieut. D.F. Charlton (killed) and 2nd Lieut. A. Dobson (prisoner), and about 20 men. For his action Capt. J.F.G. Aubin, M.C., was awarded the D.S.O.

When all the Companies had been assembled on the west of the river a line was formed, along with the remnants of another Division, overlooking the marshes. By this time the day's fighting had died down, and things remained fairly quiet throughout the night.

Early on the following morning, the 24th March, orders were received to withdraw the Battalion to Foucaucourt. The Companies were therefore assembled on the road and marched back by the main Amiens-Peronne road to an old prisoners of war camp near Foucaucourt village. Further orders awaited them there to be ready to move up again, and in about two hours they were again marching eastwards. About 8 p.m. they were again in position, in reserve, in a line north-east of Estrées.

The next morning the Battalion was hurriedly assembled and moved to Genermont, south of the main road, coming under the orders of the General Commanding the 8th Division. The situation here appeared to be very serious, as the enemy was advancing rapidly. Without any very definite orders the Battalion moved in artillery formation towards Marchelepot, but before reaching it the 8th Division, who were holding the line, had retired to the railway behind the village. Gaps along the line of the railway were accordingly filled by W and Z Companies, but it soon became necessary to put in Y Company also. No further developments occurred till about 5 p.m., when Y Company on the right found that the 24th Division on their right was withdrawing to Chaulnes ridge. A defensive flank was formed, and X Company moved to the north-east of Hyencourt to deliver a counter-attack if necessary. For a couple of hours the prospect looked very black, but the enemy did not press his advantage, and about 7 p.m. orders were received to withdraw the Battalion to a line of old trenches south-east of Pressoire. Here a quiet night was spent, with only a few casualties from shell fire.

About 9 a.m. the next day the enemy renewed his attacks and a hurried withdrawal of the whole of the 8th Division was ordered. The instructions which reached the Battalion were somewhat confused, but along with the Battalions of the 24th Infantry Brigade they moved from the trenches in artillery formation, and passing through the ruins of Lihons—which was under observation, and consequently was heavily shelled as the men passed through it—continued the withdrawal almost to Rosières. About a mile south-east of that village a line was formed, but no further attack took place. In this position the Battalion had the 2nd Northants on its left and a Labour Battalion on its right.

At 9.30 a.m. the next day (the 27th) the Labour Battalion withdrew and forced the two forward Companies of the Battalion to do the same. A counter-attack was delivered, however, and the line restored by the end of the day. The enemy renewed his attacks on the following morning, and the 24th Division on the right retired to Warvillers. Y Company then moved to Vrely to cover the withdrawal of the remainder of the Battalion to a line near Caix. It was during these operations that Lieut.-Col. F.W. Robson, D.S.O., was killed. He had commanded the Battalion for nearly a year, and could truly claim that he had realised his ambition of making it one of the finest in France. The best type of the Territorial officer, his death was a personal loss to every officer and man who served under him. The same day Capt. H. Walton, M.C., commanding Z Company, was also killed.

The three Companies in the Caix valley occupied a wired trench facing Rosières, and were told that the troops in front would retire and occupy the line with them. Instead, however, these troops passed through them, and the whole line fell back to the wood south-east of Caix. Here the remains of the Battalion were re-organised, and going forward again, re-occupied the Caix line. For this action Capt. G.E. Cardew and 2nd Lieut. R. Wilson received the Military Cross.

It was found impossible to hold the line much longer, and about 4 p.m. the Battalion withdrew along the Beaucourt road and received verbal instructions to move to Moreuil. The cooks, storemen, buglers, etc., who had been left behind when the Battalion had moved up on the 21st March, and had since been in action as part of a composite battalion, had been collected by Major T.B. Heslop, and with some stragglers were now at Ailly-sur-Noye. These were ordered up to the line on the 29th and moved to Demuin Wood, where they arrived after having marched 30 kilometres over congested roads during the previous 20 hours. They remained in the area for several days, and had a very strenuous time with several casualties. After this party had moved up, stragglers were collected by Capt. Aubin at Boves, and these, with the transport, moved by stages to Saleux, passing large numbers of French troops moving up to check the advance. At Saleux the remnants of the Division, except the details who were still in the line, were re-organised in case of emergency, and eventually entrained to Rue and marched to billets at Vron. Here Major Heslop and his party rejoined. These billets were not far from the coast, and it was expected that after the strenuous fortnight there would be a short rest. This was not to be, however, but, as an alternative, rumour suggested a tour of duty in an easy part of the line. This appeared to be confirmed when after two days the Battalion moved by 'bus to the Bethune area.

Second Phase.

On debussing just west of Bethune, the Battalion marched through the town to billets at Beuvry, which was about four miles behind one of the quietest sectors on the British front. Here a draft of about 400 men arrived, and preparations were being made for a relief of the 55th Division near La Bassée. These arrangements, however, were not carried out, and after a few days the Battalion moved by a short railway journey to Estaires, where it occupied billets in the town, all the officers—except the Commanding Officer, Adjutant, Transport Officer and Capt. Cardew—being in one billet, the Convent. At this time Estaires, though a very short distance behind the line, was a flourishing town.

After a quiet day and night, alarming rumours of the second German offensive spread, and the next night there was a "stand-to." The day following, the officers and a few N.C.O.'s reconnoitred a line of posts in support which were to be occupied in the event of an attack, and in the evening instructions were received for a relief of the Portuguese Division, which was holding the line, the relief to take place the night after (9th April).

On the night of the 8th April, there was another "stand-to," and at 4 a.m. the threatened attack commenced with a heavy bombardment of the town. One of the first shells burst in the Convent, and all the occupants with two exceptions became casualties. The men, however, got out of their billets in safety, and the highest praise is due to the N.C.O.'s, who gave valuable assistance to the three surviving Company Officers in getting the Battalion into its battle positions in the Cockshy, Marais East and West, and Drumiez posts. Amongst the officers killed in the Convent were Capt. G. Kirkhouse, Capt. J.F.G. Aubin, D.S.O., M.C., and Lieut. C.L. Tyerman, all of whom had seen much service with the Battalion.

The morning was misty, and beyond the fact that the Portuguese were being driven back in confusion, nothing definite could be ascertained as to the situation. The first reports which reached the Commanding Officer (Major T.B. Heslop) were to the effect that three Companies (W, X and Z) had been completely overwhelmed, and that two of his three Company Officers, Capt. Cardew (killed) and 2nd Lieut. Railton (prisoner) were casualties. The remainder of the Battalion, however, under Lieut. A.N. Brown, held its ground till the afternoon, when it was forced to withdraw to the railway near La Gorgue.

At dusk, orders were received to cross the river Lawe and to hold the Western bank. This withdrawal was successful, and the opportunity was taken to reorganise the Battalion, which was divided into two companies, one under Lieut. Brown, with Sergt. P. Finn, M.M., and Sergt. Field; and the other under C.S.M. T. Sordy, M.C., with Sergts. Bell and Cooper. The strength of the Battalion was now barely 100, and when touch had been established on the flanks it was found that it was holding a frontage of about 2,000 yards.

Assistance was therefore asked for, and a company of the Corps Cyclists and a company of the 7th Durham Light Infantry were attached. The latter were sent to fill a gap on the right flank between the Battalion and a Battalion of the Black Watch (51st Division). It was now about 10 a.m. on the 10th April, and the enemy had renewed his attack and gained a footing in Lestrem. From this, however, he was driven by the 7th Durham Light Infantry company, but further to the south he had pressed back the Highlanders.

Orders were then received to withdraw in a N.W. direction to the line of the Lys canal, the company of 7th Durham Light Infantry being moved over to the left flank to fill a gap which had been caused by the readjustment of their line by the 5th Durham Light Infantry. Meanwhile, the 8th Durham Light Infantry, which was in rear, was ordered up to occupy the line between the right flank of the Battalion and the 51st Division.

The new position was being fairly well held when it was reported that the 5th Durham Light Infantry on the left had been forced to retire. Both flanks being now uncertain, the Battalion was withdrawn towards Merville, under very heavy machine-gun fire. A stand was made on the outskirts of the town, but before night the fighting was taking place in the streets of the town.

The next day the retirement continued towards the Forêt de Nieppe, and a line was taken up near Le Sart. By this time the strength of the Battalion was very small, and with the remnants of the 8th Durham Light Infantry, a composite battalion was formed under Lieut.-Col. P. Kirkup, M.C. Eventually, all were withdrawn from the fighting, and moved to the grounds of La Motte Château, where they came under very heavy shell fire for a short time. For a few days longer they remained on the western edge of the Forest and provided working parties on new trenches in the forest itself on a line in front of the Rue des Morts. At the end of this time they were taken out to billets at Cohem, near Wittes, where they remained for about a week reorganising and cleaning. Here Lieut.-Col. F. Walton, M.C., returned and took over command of the Battalion from Major T.B. Heslop, who was subsequently awarded the D.S.O. for his services whilst in command. Other honours gained in the Lys battle were the Military Cross by Lieut. A.N. Brown, the bar to the Military Cross by C.S.M. T. Sordy, M.C., the D.C.M. by Sergt. P. Finn, and Military Medals by Sergts. Bell and Cooper.

Having now shared in two great battles within a month, a rest was confidently expected, and very soon orders were received to move by 'bus to Lapugnoy, near Bethune, to entrain for an unknown destination, though rumour suggested somewhere near Paris.

Third Phase.

After a twenty-four hours' journey, the Battalion detrained at Serzy, and marched to a hut camp at Arcis-le-Ponsart. Maps were scarce, but it was found that this village was somewhere east of Soissons, and that the nearest part of the line was the famous Chemin des Dames. The men of the Division were the first British troops to visit these parts, and the limited knowledge of the French language which they had found sufficient in

Belgium and the North was found to be useless. Other Divisions were expected to come South, but for a short time the 50th occupied the unique position of being the only British troops in the Sixth French Army.

In the camp at Arcis-le-Ponsart were all the battalions of the 151st Brigade, and the ceremony of Brigade guard mounting was revived. This took place daily in the centre of the village with the massed buglers and bands. On the occasion of a visit of the French Army Commander to Divisional Headquarters, a guard was provided at very short notice by the Battalion, and was complimented on its smart appearance and bearing. It may be mentioned that the bugler of this guard carried the silver bugle presented to the Battalion in 1861 by the ladies of Coundon.

It was generally understood that the tour on this sector, which was one of the quietest in the line, was to be a period of rest and training prior to a return to the fighting further north. Accordingly, the days at Arcis were devoted to training, mostly in field work. The men whose training was not up to standard, including a certain number who had recently been transferred from the Inland Water Transport section of the Royal Engineers, were detached for separate instruction, and eventually went to form a Divisional School.

After about three weeks' training, during which an epidemic of influenza visited the camp, the Battalion marched to billets in Glennes, a small village near the Aisne. Here final preparations were made for the line, and after a few days it moved up to relieve a battalion of the 73rd French Infantry Regiment in the woods immediately east of the Craonne Plateau.

The relief was very interesting. Arriving in the woods in the dark, the men were led by French guides by bewildering tracks and trenches to the front line. When daylight came, the support companies found themselves amidst green trees, very different surroundings from those they had previously known as the forward area. To add to the general comfort there were practically no indications that the war was still on. The shelling consisted at the most of half-a-dozen explosions daily, and generally there was "nothing doing." The rations came up to Battalion Headquarters by train, and the carrying parties lost their terrors.

After four days the Battalion moved out to the support area, which consisted of billets in the deserted village of Chaudardes. Here concerts were organised, there was bathing in the Aisne Canal, the band played selections in the centre of the village, and it was even possible to do a certain amount of training when the enemy's observation balloons were not up.

The four days in support being finished, a return was made to the line, this time on the right sub-sector, with the 8th Durham Light Infantry on the left. The conditions were still good, and everything pointed to this being a rest sector for the enemy also.

Nothing unusual occurred till the evening of the 26th May, when a message was received to the effect that a prisoner had stated that after a three-hours' bombardment the enemy was going to attack at 4 a.m. on the 27th. Observers also reported that towards dusk the roads behind the enemy's line were black with troops. The situation appeared to be so improbable that it was difficult to regard it as serious. The necessary precautions were taken, however; reserves of ammunition were sent forward, surplus personnel were sent down to the transport lines, and everybody warned to be on the alert.

Promptly at 1 a.m. on the 27th the barrage came down, and it was such as had never been experienced by the Battalion before. The enemy flooded the whole area to a depth of about 3,000 yards with high explosive, shrapnel, and gas shells. Even the stores and transport, as was afterwards disclosed, were shelled out of Muscourt, which was many miles back, south of the Aisne.

Communication with the forward companies was maintained by telephone, and an occasional runner, and at 4.50 a.m. a message was received at Headquarters from the front line stating that the enemy had attacked in force and had overwhelmed the forward posts. An enemy tank was also reported to be tearing up the wire. The next information came from Capt. Lyon who, finding his Company (X) had been wiped out, reported at Battalion Headquarters that the enemy was advancing rapidly. The reserve company (Z), under Capt. R. Green, M.C., were in position close to Headquarters, and they reported the enemy on top of them, with machine guns behind their right flank and bombers behind their left.

It was then decided to move Headquarters further to the rear, and it was afterwards discovered that at this time parties of the enemy were actually well in rear of the position.

After moving down the communication trench for about 500 yards, Lieut.-Col. Walton, with the Adjutant and Signalling Officer, and Capt. Lyon, collected all the available men, about forty of the Battalion, and searched for the best place to make a stand. They were still under the barrage, and the smoke made matters very difficult. Presently the 5th Durham Light Infantry came up the trench to take up an allotted position, which they found to be already taken by the enemy. They moved off to the right of the main trench, however, and the forty men under Capt. Lyon joined them.

A message was then received by the Commanding Officer telling him to report at Brigade Headquarters. On arrival, however, the dug-outs were found to be unoccupied. Enemy machine guns were now firing from the rear, and it was realised that apart from about half-a-dozen orderlies who formed the remains of the Headquarters personnel, the Battalion had been practically annihilated.

In his search for the Brigadier, who, it afterwards transpired, had been killed, Lieut.-Col. Walton arrived at the bridge at Concevreux. Here he found a few men of the 8th Durham Light Infantry and the 5th Northumberland Fusiliers, with whom the bridge was held till the afternoon. Unfortunately, none of the Battalion joined this party from the front, and for the next two or three days the two Commanding Officers of the 6th and 8th Durham Light Infantry found themselves in command of various bodies of men of other battalions.

Meanwhile those of the Battalion who were at the transport lines when the battle started had been collected on the road from Muscourt to Romain under Major T.B. Heslop, D.S.O., and placed under the orders of the G.O.C. 74th Brigade. Whilst on the road they could see enemy troops and guns on the far side of the Aisne valley and later saw these guns being fired point blank at them. Various positions were taken up during the day, the party being in close contact with the enemy and suffering many casualties. On the 29th these details, which had rejoined the transport, were ordered to move from Villers Argon to Baslieux-sous-Chatillon, but before reaching the latter place, every available man was again collected to form part of a Company under Major Heslop, representing the remnants of the 151st Brigade in a Battalion to which each Brigade of the Division contributed one Company. After a night in Quisles Château this Battalion moved towards Ville-en-Tardenois to support the 74th Brigade. The enemy's position was uncertain and the 151st Brigade Company were ordered to act as advance guard and to seize the high ground north and east of Romigny. This was done, but the enemy attacked in force, with the result that the Company were driven to a position south of the village which they held till reinforcements arrived.

Eventually, the remnants of the Division, except the Composite Battalion, were assembled at Vert-la-Gravelle, south of the Marne, when a Composite Brigade was formed, consisting of a weak Battalion from each of the original Brigades. This Brigade, after about a week spent in reorganisation, moved up to Chaumuzy and the Bois de Courton, where it did good work in a counter-attack on the Bligny ridge. Meanwhile, the transport and stores moved back to Broyes, near Sezanne, where they were eventually joined by the members of the Composite Battalion. For actions during the whole of the operations, the Military Cross was awarded to Capt. A.B. Hare, Lieut. T.

Rushworth, 2nd Lieut. J. Woodhead, and R.S.M. J. Taylor. The last named was wounded and was succeeded by C.S.M. T. Sordy, M.C. The Military Medal was awarded to Sergt. Malone, L.-Cpl. Ripley and Pte. Dinsley, and the French Croix de Guerre to Corpl. Nield.

At Broyes still another Composite Battalion was formed from the Brigade in case of emergency, and though orders were received to proceed into the line, they were cancelled.

Then came the news that owing to the military demands, the 50th Division was to be broken up. Nothing definite, however, could be ascertained, and early in June the remnants entrained at Sezanne for the Abbeville area. On detraining at Longpre they marched to billets at Caumont, where orders were received that the battalions were to be reduced to the strength of Training Cadres (10 officers and 50 other ranks). After a few days they marched to Warcheville, from where the surplus men (about 120) were sent to the Base. It may be mentioned that the total casualties in the Battalion during the months of March, April and May had been 60 officers and over 1,200 other ranks.

In a few more days the Battalion, now a Training Cadre, moved by 'bus to a camp just outside Dieppe, and there a month was spent awaiting further orders. The time was spent in the training of the N.C.O.'s who were to be instructors on special subjects, and in visits to the town. The band had been lent to the 50th Division, which had been filled up by new battalions from Salonica and was able to play selections in the camp, and on one occasion in the town.

At the end of the month's stay, about the middle of August, it was announced that the battalions were not to be disbanded, but retained for training purposes. A few days later the Cadres of the 5th, 6th and 8th Durham Light Infantry moved by train to Rouen, where they were to build a camp and start a new institution, that of instructing reinforcement officers at the Base in tactical schemes. The officers of the Cadres therefore began the latter work, whilst the N.C.O.'s and men worked, or superintended the work on the new camp. In this somewhat monotonous way two months dragged on, during which, in the temporary absence on sick leave of Lieut.-Col. Walton, Lieut.-Col. Montgomerie, M.C., of the Norfolk Regiment, was in command. The band still remained with the Battalion and after the Armistice was granted permission to play on the Joan of Arc statue, being the first British band to do so. They also had the unique experience of playing "Blaydon Races" in Rouen Cathedral.

About the middle of October came rumours of the splitting up of the Cadres, and on the 18th October Lieut.-Col. Walton was ordered to proceed to take command of the 18th Durham Light Infantry. He was succeeded by Lieut.-Col. A.L. MacMillan of the Seaforth Highlanders, who commanded, however, for only a few days, for on the 6th November the Battalion was demobilised, and within a few days the personnel had been scattered to various battalions all over France.

So within a few days of the Armistice, ended the career of the 6th Durham Light Infantry in France, after three and a half years of good work which had made for it, right up to the end, a reputation which bore not a single stain, and which on more than one occasion had caused it to be held up as an example of the efficiency of the Territorial Force to which it had the great honour to belong.

APPENDICES.

APPENDIX I.
OFFICERS KILLED OR DIED.

Major S.E. Badcock

Capt. T.J. Monkhouse   }   26th April, 1915.

2nd Lieut. C.S. Kynoch

2nd Lieut. J.M. Hare   24th May, 1915.

2nd Lieut. G.C. Robertson   21st July, 1915.

2nd Lieut. L.M. Peberdy   22nd Dec., 1915.

2nd Lieut. L. Meyer   11th June, 1916.

2nd Lieut. R.J. Harris   16th June, 1916.

2nd Lieut. J.C. Miller   27th July, 1916.

2nd Lieut. H.C. Annett   15th Sept., 1916.

2nd Lieut. N.F. Charlton   18th Sept., 1916.

2nd Lieut. W. Little   1st Oct., 1916.

2nd Lieut. D.R. Peacock   2nd Oct., 1916.

2nd Lieut. C.H.B. Catford[A]   5th Oct., 1916.

2nd Lieut. G.W. Robson

2nd Lieut. A.S. Ritson   }

2nd Lieut. S. Robson

2nd Lieut. T.F. Applegarth	5th Nov., 1916.
2nd Lieut. K.B. Stuart	
2nd Lieut. H. Fell	
Major W.D. Carswell Hunt, M.C.[B]	5th April, 1917.
Capt. A.L. Brock	
Lieut. W.H. Richardson	
2nd Lieut. J.W. Payne	} 14th April, 1917.
2nd Lieut. H. Greener	
2nd Lieut. W.L. Newton	
2nd Lieut. D.D.R. Lewis[A]	22nd April, 1917.
Lieut. D.F. Charlton	24th March, 1918.
2nd Lieut. T. Sharkey	}
2nd Lieut. A.R. Burn	26th March, 1918.
Capt. H. Walton, M.C.	
Lieut. T.J. Burton[A]	} 27th March, 1918.
Lieut.-Col. F.W. Robson, D.S.O.	
2nd Lieut. A.A. Horwood	28th March, 1918.
Capt. J.F.G. Aubin, D.S.O., M.C.	
Capt. G.E. Cardew, M.C.	}
Capt. G. Kirkhouse	

Capt. Mackenzie (R.A.M.C.)[A]

Lieut. C.L. Tyerman   9th April, 1918.

Lieut. D.B. Scott

2nd Lieut. R.A. Wilson, M.C.

2nd Lieut. F. Shirtliffe

Capt. W.B. Hansell
                                                        }
Capt. A.N. Brown, M.C.   27th May, 1918.

2nd Lieut. J.C. Garritt.   30th May, 1918.

[A] Died of wounds.

[B] Died.

APPENDIX II.

(The ranks shown are the highest held by the respective officers during their service in France.)

COMMANDING OFFICERS.

Lieut.-Col. H.C. Watson	19th April-28th April, 1915.
Lieut.-Col. J.W. Jeffreys, D.S.O.	28th April-19th May, 1915.
Major W.E. Taylor (York and Lancaster Regt.).	19th May-24th May, 1915.
Lieut.-Col. J.W. Jeffreys, D.S.O.	24th May-11th Aug., 1915.[C]
Brig.-Gen. O.C. Borrett, C.M.G., D.S.O. (King's Own Regt.).	11th Aug.-15th Aug., 1915.
Lieut.-Col. J.W. Jeffreys, D.S.O.	15th Aug.-19th Dec.,

1915.

Brig.-Gen. G.A. Stevens, C.M.G., D.S.O. (Royal Fusiliers).	19th Dec., 1915-27th April, 1916.
Lieut.-Col. J.W. Jeffreys, D.S.O.	27th April,-23rd Sept., 1916.
Major G.E. Wilkinson, M.C. (Northumberland Fusiliers).	23rd Sept.-1st Oct., 1916.
Brig.-Gen. R.B. Bradford, V.C., M.C.	1st Oct.-2nd Oct., 1916.
Lieut.-Col. A. Ebsworth, M.C., D.C.M. (East Lancashire Regt.).	2nd Oct.-6th Nov., 1916.
Lieut.-Col. H.M. Allen, C.M.G., D.S.O. (Black Watch).	6th Nov., 1916-Feb., 1917.
Lieut.-Col. J.W. Jeffreys, D.S.O.	Feb.-25th March, 1917.

(During this period the command was held for short intervals by Lieut.-Col. W.B. Little, D.S.O., M.C. (East Lancashire Regt.), and Lieut.-Col. E. Crouch, D.S.O., D.C.M. during the temporary absence in hospital of Lieut.-Col. Jeffreys.)

Major W.D. Carswell Hunt. M.C.	25th March-5th April, 1917.
Lieut.-Col. A. Ebsworth, M.C., D.C.M.	5th April-11th April, 1917.
Lieut.-Col. F.W. Robson, D.S.O., (Yorkshire Regt.).	11th April, 1917-27th Mar., 1918.
Lieut.-Col. T.B. Heslop, D.S.O.	27th March-April, 1918.
Lieut.-Col. F. Walton, M.C.	April-18th Oct., 1918.

(During this period the command was held for a few days by Lieut.-Col. E.W. Montgomerie, M.C. (Norfolk Regt.), during the temporary absence of

Lieut.-Col. Walton.)

Lieut.-Col. A.L. MacMillan (Seaforth Highlanders).   18th Oct.-6th Nov., 1918.

ADJUTANTS.

Lieut.-Col. J.W. Jeffreys, D.S.O.   19th April-28th April, 1915.

Lieut. R.V. Hare   28th April-19th May, 1915.

Lieut.-Col. J.W. Jeffreys, D.S.O.   19th May-24th May, 1915.

Capt. P.H.B. Lyon, M.C.   24th May-20th Dec., 1915.[C]

Brig.-Gen. R.B. Bradford, V.C., M.C.   20th Dec.-31st Dec., 1915.

Lieut. C.E.G. Yaldwyn   31st Dec., 1915-May, 1916.

Capt. G. Kirkhouse   May-20th Sept., 1916.

Lieut.-Col. A. Ebsworth, M.C., D.C.M.   20th Sept.-2nd Oct., 1916

Capt. G. Kirkhouse   2nd Oct.-10th Nov., 1916.

Lieut. T.J. Arnott (Gordon Highlanders)   10th Nov., 1916-5th April, 1917.

Major G.D.R. Dobson, M.C.   5th April-3rd May, 1917.

Capt. R.B. Ainsworth, M.C.   3rd May, 1917-6th Nov., 1918.

QUARTERMASTER.

Capt. W.M. Hope, M.C.   19th April, 1915-6th Nov., 1918.

(With short interval when wounded in 1918.)

TRANSPORT OFFICER.

Lieut. H.T. Bircham, M.C.   19th April, 1915-June, 1918.[C]

[C] With interval from 8th June-11th Aug., 1915 during the amalgamation of the 6th and 8th Battalions.

APPENDIX III

(The ranks shown are the highest held by the respective officers during their service in France.)

DECORATIONS WON BY OFFICERS SERVING WITH THE BATTALION.

D.S.O.

- Lieut.-Col. J.W. Jeffreys.
- Lieut.-Col. T.B. Heslop.
- Capt. J.F.G. Aubin.

M.C. & BAR.

- Capt. J.F.G. Aubin.

M.C.

- Lieut.-Col. F. Walton.
- Capt. T. Welch.
- Capt. R.H. Wharrier.
- Capt. H. Walton.
- Capt. R.S. Johnson.
- Capt. R.B. Ainsworth.
- Capt. P.H.B. Lyon.
- Capt. W.M. Hope.
- Capt. G.E. Cardew.
- Capt. A.N. Brown.
- Capt. T. Rushworth.
- Capt. A.B. Hare.
- Lieut. W.P. Gill.
- Lieut. G.R. Angus.

- Lieut. B.J. Harvey.

- Lieut. H.T. Bircham.

- 2nd Lieut. R.A. Wilson.

- 2nd Lieut. J. Woodhead.

The V.C. was won by Brig.-Genl. R.B. Bradford whilst in command of the 6th and 9th Battalions.

Milton Keynes UK
Ingram Content Group UK Ltd.
UKHW032014161124
451262UK00019B/750